A SMALL B〔...〕RSE

*(Well, a large book would be
much worse)*

by

Gillian Hart

Edited by Lucy Davis

Dedicated to my grandchildren,

Amy, Josie, Lucy, and Ryan.

Remember, a grandmother is just for Christmas –
not forever.

<u>What is poetry?</u>

A rhyming ditty:

Sometimes dark, sometimes witty.

A couplet or more wordy rhyme –

Many have withstood the sands of time.

Some poetry is a picture

Painted in words

CONTENTS

TRADITION AND BELIEF

FOOD AND COOKING

AGE

HISTORY AND POLITICS

CITY AND COUNTRY

HUMOUR

LIVING IN LOCKDOWN

FAMILY AND FRIENDS

A Child

When you have a child,

It is for life –

Not always so with a husband or a wife.

The arrival of that small person changes everything

From day one –

Suddenly it seems life is no longer fun.

Broken nights,

Disrupted days

Life seems to be lived in a permanent haze.

Until one day you get a toothless smile –

Suddenly every change and every upheaval seems worthwhile.

Kids

"It wasn't me! It was him! It isn't fair!"

Oh! What an annoying, squabbling pair!

Peaceful times were fairly rare.

When they loved each other and played together

They were as unpredictable as our weather.

But as they grew up peace reigned

And from their closeness, each one gained.

They no longer said, *"it's not fair"* –

Although in adulthood they've learned

That fairness in life is very rare.

A New Year Resolution

Mummy, I promise to be good

As you've always said I should.

I won't hit my dear little brother (well, not too much),

And if I do it will be with a much lighter touch.

I won't hide my vegetables in the big plant pot,

'Cos they smell so awful when they begin to rot.

I won't keep on ringing our neighbour's bell,

For last time, when running away, he told me to go to hell –

And I fell.

I won't lock the garden door,

So my dear little brother is left outside when it starts to pour.

Well, so far so good, but it's only day one –

And I can see that life's not going to be much fun.

A Special Friend

"I am your daddy's Special Friend," she said,

As I stared up at her face from my little bed.

Gently she stroked a straying curl,

"Soon you will be my little girl."

Suddenly she swooped and held me close to her pointed chest –

It wasn't soft and warm like my mummy's breast.

And then I remembered how I cried that cold, wet, rainy day

When those men in black coats took my mummy away.

The Mask (Sequel to 'A Special Friend')

In public she was kind and caring,
In private she was cold and distant.

I learned as a child
It was best to stay out of her way –
And that I did,
Growing up, day after day.

She was my father's second wife
She had a beautiful home and a luxurious life.
In public she always wore a smile –
Then one day, the mask slipped

My father died –
She didn't shed a tear –
She never cried.

She told me he was "*an old so and so,*"
She told me things about their life together
I didn't need or want to know.

So, I left my family home –

The last time I saw her she was sitting in the lounge

All alone!

Many years later I had a change of heart:

I went and brought this old, frail woman to my home.

She loved my children and said they were her life –

It's a pity she didn't feel the same about me

When she was my father's wife!

Delivery

"*I HATE YOU!*" she shouted at her husband.

He sat in the corner of the room.

He had already been outside to have a sandwich and a drink –

"*Darling,*" he said,

"*That's not what you really think.*"

"*It is,*" she said,

"*I've been here for hours with awful pain –*

Oh God! Here it is again!"

The midwife said, "*One last push and your baby will be here.*"

Suddenly everything was clear.

The room was filled with morning light –

It had certainly been 'A Hard Day's Night'!

Their baby lay across her chest

Her husband said, "*I've had a worrying night,*

But everything is now alright."

Proudly he looked at their baby and said,

"*The first in our family.*"

She looked up at him and said,

"*Fine, you can have the next one instead!*"

Good News

It was midnight when the call came through –
It couldn't be good news, I somehow knew.

The voice was faint and sounded far away –
I was tense waiting to hear what the caller had to say.
My imagination worked over-time, my heart full of dread,
I waited nervously to hear what my son said.

"Don't worry, Mum – we wanted you to be the first to know,
We've decided to give that old-fashioned institution a go.
We're getting married –
Your granddaughters are going to be bridesmaids at last."
Suddenly all my premonitions were in the past.

Mother's Day

Holding a new baby makes your 'Mother's Day'.

The first time you leave that little person at the school gate

Ensuring they won't be late,

That's a Mother's Day.

When you watch that young adult receive a degree –

Your pride is there for all to see

(Another Mother's Day)

At the wedding when they become husband and wife,

Which you hope will be for life,

That's another Mother's Day.

And when you hold that first grandchild close to your heart,

Hoping you'll be able to play a part,

That's Grandmother's Day.

My Grandfather

The old man sat in the armchair,

The early morning sun glistening on his silver hair.

He was smartly dressed in his best suit:

His grandson was going to take him out for the day –

He smiled at the thought

Of seeing his great-grandchildren at play.

His mind drifted back to when he arrived in England

At nineteen years old,

Not knowing how his life would unfold.

He worked hard, married, raised a family,

With many pleasures and hardships on the way.

Now all he had to do was sit and wait –

Always on time, he was never late.

The little girls skipped into the room,

"*Grandpa, Grandpa*," they cried out.

Their father following them took one look –

He had no doubt –

He put them quietly back in the hall,

"*I must attend to Grandpa, he's had a fall.*"

But he knew that the old man had been waiting for this moment

Without fear,

To join so many he had held dear.

It wasn't the time to shed a tear.

Christmas Day 1976

The Light of Life

Life is like a candle flame,

Sometimes on wax, sometimes on wane.

In the beginning it is soft and light,

Its hold is tenuous, so very slight.

Then it grows stronger, more upright –

Gaining strength, character, and height.

It seems little can reduce this flame –

Until, one day, nothing is the same.

So it was with my mother's life:

A wonderful daughter, mother, and wife.

A light went out in the lives of all who knew her,

And many shed a tear

At the loss of someone so very dear.

My Best Friend

My best friend is dead.

I've cried so much; my eyes are sore and red.

My heart still beats but feels like lead.

I know that warm, sunny days lie ahead –

But what do I care, for my best friend is dead.

He was only seventeen and I thought only had a bad leg –

He still followed me round the room with adoring eyes,

But could no longer sit up and beg.

The vet said it was cruel to keep him alive –

He would never get better, could never thrive.

And so my dog, my best friend, is dead.

Touch Me Not

He gently touched my knee,
Then wandered up my thigh.

I gave him a stern look
And uttered a reproachful sigh.

Suddenly he was lying on his back,
Stretched across my lap.

I looked into his eyes, so deep and green –
What did this latest move mean?

Then I remembered and gently stroked his tummy.
His whiskers twitched, he purred with glee
George, the cat, thought he'd got the best of me.

Cat

Message from my son:

Don't forget to feed the cat

Otherwise he'll be leaving dead mice on the mat.

Presents

Most of us have done it, I'm as guilty as the rest:

Recycling unwanted gifts, just keeping the best.

Chocolates, you should watch the sell-by date –

You can't pass them on when it's too late.

When my cousin got engaged she received a hideous glass bowl

She wanted to go out into the garden and dig it into a hole.

Instead, she kept it for a while before sending it on its way,

Never giving it a thought for many a day.

Until her younger sister got engaged

And there on the table in a brand-new pack

Was that hideous glass bowl!

It had returned to her family – it had come back.

Inside the bowl was a card which said,

"*Best wishes to Vera and John.*"

Vera and John!

They hadn't even changed the card before they passed it on.

Three Girls

Faith was a pious young woman:

She liked to read and quote from the Good Book.

Her aims in life were to get married, have children,

And learn to be a good cook.

Her friend Hope lived life in a constant whirl –

Tomorrow would always be a better day

And this was the maxim she lived by, come what may!

Then there was Charity:

Charity was a kind and friendly girl,

Especially to elderly rich men

(It was said she had already been kind to a lot of them).

She had a nice house, a good lifestyle, and a snazzy sports car –

She was a girl that intended to go far.

Faith, Hope, and Charity: three very different young women

But they had been friends from childhood

And would be friends throughout life.

They were always there to support each other

In good times, bad times, times of trouble and strife.

Handout

A 'handout' often means

Giving someone something you don't really need,

So it cannot really be called a good deed.

To receive a handout sounds demeaning

There is a phrase with a far better meaning.

That is a 'hand out-stretched' –

In friendship, sympathy, compassion, comfort, love.

A hand out-stretched to someone in need,

Now that is certainly a good deed.

RELATIONSHIPS

My First Kiss

I was fourteen years old,

He a spotty fifteen-year-old.

My friends said he fancied me,

It was obvious for all to see.

Our first date was a cinema matinee –

My mother said I mustn't be home late.

We went to see E.T., it was very sad

I sat and cried – I think he thought I was mad.

He grew bolder,

His arm snaked round my shoulder.

He turned my head to plant a kiss –

I jerked away – it was a definite miss.

Later on, he tried again –

It was a bit better

Although it reminded me of being kissed by our dog,

A slobbery red setter.

April Fool

They met in February.
She was young, vibrant, and full of fun
When he was with her he felt dazzled,
As if sitting in the sun.

She told him she didn't think of him as being old –
What she didn't tell him was that to her
His bank account was a pot of gold.

By March, most of his money had been spent
So she found a younger, richer model,
And off she went.

In April, he decided to go back home –
He'd apologise to his wife
And say he'd never again roam.

He stood on the doorstep looking dejected and sad
His wife opened the door and said, "*I'm not mad.
I'm not your April Fool,
And I don't want to see or speak to you anymore.*"
And with that she firmly shut the door.

Postscript:

Their neighbour stood behind the garden wall.

He thought, "*I'll wait a couple of days,*

Then I'll give her a call."

Dead Flowers

His flowers are dead, they didn't last.

Just like his love, all in the past.

I came downstairs early next morning

I hadn't slept all night – I couldn't stop yawning.

I looked through the open living room door

My favourite vase lay shattered on the floor.

I sat amongst the shards of glass and cried –

I felt as if my heart had died.

Suddenly the phone rang.

His voice was soft and very low,

"*I'm sorry,*" he said, "*I really do love you, you know.*

Can I come round tomorrow night?"

Suddenly the world was set to right.

Waiting

I waited by the bus stop
I waited at the station for your train,
You never came.

I waited outside your house one day
Until a neighbour told me you had gone away –
Still you never came.

I cried myself to sleep on many a night –
I lost so much weight, I looked a sight
And still you never came.

So this was to be my fate,
Endless feelings of love or hate.
Still you never came.

Months passed, then one day you stood outside my door.
Your smiling face, the lies on your lips,
They cut me to my core.

But you came back.

I rushed out through the open door,

Hit you so hard you landed on the floor.

Shutting you out of my life –

I knew you wouldn't come back anymore.

A Good Yarn

The old couple sat in their garden,

Enjoying the evening warmth.

They sat contentedly, side by side.

"Do you remember when I came here as your bride,

You used to sit and look into my eyes?"

"Yes, dear", the old man said obligingly,

Looking in her eyes – they looked a bit sore and red –

"Do you remember how you used to lovingly stroke my arm?"

"Yes, dear, but then it wasn't covered in anti-rheumatic balm!"

"Do you remember how you used to nibble my ear?"

The old man got up and went towards the house –

"Where are you going, dear?"

"I'm going to put my teeth in, but I'll be back, never fear!"

Broken Heart

My alter-ego, my partner for life:

You were my husband,

I was your wife.

There was nothing in our life together you could not mend,

Except my broken heart

When too soon the time came,

We had to part.

TRADITION AND BELIEF

A Journey

My mother packed my suitcase,

It was small and brown.

"*Soon,*" she said,

"*You will be going to live in another town.*

Your father will take you on a train,"

I looked up at her face,

It was full of pain.

"*Then you will be going on a boat.*

It will be cold –

You'd better wear your warmest coat."

I asked, "*Will Papa be going on that boat too?*"

"*No, my darling,*

But there will be many children just like you."

Now I am old and have children and grandchildren of my own,

I can contact them anywhere in the world by internet or phone.

But of my family and friends long dead

All I have are the memories in my head.

Oh yes, and I still have that suitcase, small and brown,

The one my mother packed

When I left my country, my home, and my town.

The Gift

The bell rang and I opened the door.

An elderly woman stood there, neatly pressed,

But obviously poor.

She asked for me by a name I hadn't heard for years –

Her request brought me close to tears.

She held out a box:

"This is for you," she said.

Her accented voice quivered and she bowed her head.

"Come in,"

I ushered her into my home and we stared at each other

"Please open the box,

The contents belonged to your mother."

The golden chain with a diamond drop shone

As I held it to the light,

Memories flooded back of my mother wearing it

To go out at night.

"A lifetime ago I worked for your family, they were good to me.

Your father gave the necklace into my care

Before they tried to flee.

I knew you had got to England when a few were able to leave –

I didn't know what was going to happen,

This you must believe."

She touched my hand gently and went away.

I never saw her again from that day.

Dumplings

My grandma was known as the Kneidlach Queen:
Her dumplings were so light and white,
They added to the joy of many a festival and Friday night.

This tradition, my mother took over
Her kneidlach floated majestically in the soup,
Like the white cliffs of Dover.

Then I got married, and my first Friday night
The table set, the candles alight,
I sat at my new dining table,
The kneidlach nestling in my ladle.

I served my new husband – he took one bite and then another,
"Tomorrow," he said, *"you should phone my mother.*
She makes dumplings called Matzo Kleis,
You'll like them – they are very nice."

Into the hot soup my tears fell:
So this is marriage, a living hell.

I phoned my mother-in-law early the next day,

She told me how to make Matzo Kleis the Dutch way.

"Your husband comes from a Dutch line, you see,

Not from Russian ancestry like you and me."

So, from that time, and all these years later,

Matzo Kleis is what I cater.

Spring Cleaning

I've opened wide the windows, to let the fresh air in.

Everything surplus to requirements has been thrown in the bin.

I've washed, tidied and polished

Now everything is super clean and bright

The rabbi's bought my chametz,

The transaction took place last night.

I've cooked and baked – it's been a long, hard day –

If anyone asks me why I'm tired, what should I say?

I'm now searching for crumbs with my candle and feather –

Will I do all this again?

I tell myself never.

Well, not until next year!

Talking to God

I asked, *"Are you the one in charge,*
Who made this world and the universe so large?"

A voice rose on a sudden breeze
Soft and clear, I could hear it with ease:

"Yes, I made your world, including the human race,
Which seems to have multiplied at quite a pace.
Of all creatures, I gave you the greatest intelligence,
But I watch your actions which don't make sense.
You've fought and killed each other since time began –
I'm beginning to lose patience with the behaviour of man.
I send warnings:
Tsunamis, volcanic eruptions, earthquakes, a flood or two.
Eventually, sadly, I will have to dispose of all of you."

I sat up suddenly and began to scream –
Then I realised it was just a dream.

Adam's Apple

"Oh Lord!" said Adam,

"Here comes Eve and she's clutching that apple in her hand.

Yesterday she had a bite

And I didn't have a wink of sleep all night."

The serpent slithered down the tree –

'As you sow, so you shall reap.'

"You'd better get used to having not much sleep."

"Have you noticed Eve has put on a lot of weight?"

"Yes," said Adam,

"And she keeps on saying she's missed her usual date.

And she says we must start wearing 'clothes' –

What are they?

I've asked around but no one knows."

The serpent smiled,

"Well, in the Garden of Eden

You are the only two members of the human race,

And you will be growing at quite a pace.

Soon you will leave here to wander in the lands outside

With your ever-increasing tribe.

For centuries you'll go back and forth

Until the day you will cease to roam

For you will find a place that you can call home."

Adam wanted to ask the serpent more,

But when he looked, he had disappeared

As he'd done so many times before.

What am I?

I nestle in a box on a wooden rack

There are hundreds like me sitting back-to-back.

A man in a white coat and hat approaches carrying a light

Anxiously I wait my turn – I hope I'll be alright.

My surface is white and thin, I cannot bear the heat –

Soon I'll know my fate, if I'm good enough to eat.

What am I? Well, if I pass the test,

I am a kosher egg – one of the very best!

FOOD AND COOKING

Gadgets

In my kitchen I have a cupboard and a drawer

Brim-full of gadgets never used

Or used no more.

I have a potato ricer –

What could be nicer?

A pasta maker used twice

Until I realised shop-bought pasta was just as nice.

I have a strawberry huller

And a contraption that removes the core from a pineapple –

The leaflet says "with ease" –

Could someone show me how to use it, please?!

So, when I've cleared this cupboard and this drawer,

I'll go out to the garage

Where all the larger unwanted items are in store!

A Recipe for Happiness

I like to cook, it gives me pleasure

But I never, ever weigh or measure.

A handful of this, a handful of that,

A spoonful of this, a spoonful of that,

A sprinkling of spice –

Hmm! That tastes nice.

No wonder no dish ever turns out the same twice!

Best of all I like to make a meal for family and friends.

This I do with loving care,

Knowing it is something we're going to share.

And if it turns out a success

I call it my Recipe for Happiness!

<u>Chocolate</u>

Chocolate:

So succulent, so sophisticated, so dark brown –

It cheers you up when you are feeling down.

Chocolate can be light brown or even white,

But on some occasions this doesn't seem right.

When you are feeling below par

What you need is a dark brown chocolate bar.

A Guilty Pleasure

My friend, a rather large lady,
Was extremely fond of everything sweet –
Chocolates were her special treat.

In order to keep her in shape
Her husband forbade any confectionery in the house –
Wasn't he a thoughtful spouse!

One day she desperately hunted
High and low for something sweet
To eat –

Eventually in a bedroom drawer nestling beneath his socks
She found an unopened chocolate box.

She went and locked the bedroom door,
Then placed the chocolate box on the floor.

Chocolate coated ginger –
She liked the chocolate, but not the ginger.
Never mind, she'd better not linger.

She gently sucked the chocolate from each ginger orb,

Washed them, dried them, and replaced them in the box

Which she fitted nicely back below the socks!

AGE

A Generation Puzzle

A new language:

He is cool, she is hot and fit

Do I understand? Well, a little bit!

I ask, "*Are you well?*"

They reply they are good!

I am pleased you are good,

And so you should, be good.

Things are awesome, ledge (legendary), or boring –

The number of things that are boring seems to be soaring.

Who is that, spread out on the settee?

Earphones on, mobile in hand, and watching TV?

Why, it is my multi-tasking grandson,

Not quite linguist of the year.

I know we speak a common language

But what he says to me is not always clear!

The Movies

When I was young I saw 'Gone with the Wind' –

I admired Clark Gable and daydreamed

That one day I might change my name from Gillian Abel.

Then I heard that to film he had his ears pinned back,

And his leading ladies complained of his bad breath –

So that fancy died a natural death.

Rock Hudson was so handsome and virile as could be –

I thought he might be the man for me –

Then I realised if I gave him an alluring smile

He would probably run a mile.

Doris Day –

So vivacious and her voice so full of fun

But I was skinny, shy, and couldn't sing,

So being her look-a-like was never going to be the thing.

Hedy Lamarr – one of the most beautiful women by far,

And clever too.

Then I heard that to avoid wrinkles she never smiled,

So I quickly stopped being so beguiled.

Where are the giants of the movie screen today?

They can't hold a candle to our past idols,

I regret to say.

Spending A Penny

The small boy pressed his face against the corner shop window.

He had been given a penny to spend as a treat

And knew he would buy something sweet.

He gazed at the large glass jars standing on a shelf in a row:

Sherbet drops, liquorice sticks, humbugs,

Sugar candy, chocolate drops, coconut ice

(That looked nice)

And some he didn't know.

On the counter, lying on a cloth, were the sheets of toffee.

The lady in the shop had a little metal hammer

And divided it up in a very methodical manner.

The shop bell rang as he pushed the door –

The old man woke up from his dream –

Every night he went back to his childhood with a similar theme.

He struggled out of bed – he'd better be quick!

Shuffled to the bathroom

Nowadays he often spent a penny

At six o'clock in the morning, the first of many!

Nostalgia

When you have time to look back with pleasure
At those past moments that you treasure,
That is nostalgia.

The memory of a kiss
Holding a new-born baby in your arms – what bliss!
That is nostalgia.

Looking back down memory lane
You remember the good times, not the pain.
That is nostalgia.

Your memories are fleeting moments in the present day –
A sudden breeze can blow them away.
That is nostalgia.

Remember: what was, was, and what is, is –
Nurture nostalgia or, like champagne, it can lose its fizz!

The Past

When I was young there was no past,

Only a present to be lived each day.

Clutching at every moment to make it last

There was no December, only May.

Now the past and present merge as one

No dawn to look forward to – only the setting sun.

Reflections

I've walked the length of the high street.

I am hot, tired, and have sore feet.

Oh good, there is a seat –

I sit and gaze in the shop window across the way

There are loads of people reflected in passing on a busy day.

Suddenly, I think I know someone I can see –

Then I realise that old lady, seated, is me!

Me

Startled, I sat up and said,

"*Who are you?*"

To the young woman standing at the foot of my bed.

She was tall and slim

With brown wavy hair and big brown eyes.

She gave me a look full of surprise.

She said, "*I thought you'd know –*

I'm you, but from a long, long time ago.

I've brought with me a lot of people from your past:

Friends and family – loved ones –

The number is quite vast."

They came in through the open door

And stood on the window ledge, on the furniture –

There was no room on the floor.

They started to climb up onto my bed

I pulled the duvet over my head

And let out a scream –

And then I realised it was just a dream.

The Address Book

Sometimes when I look in my address book I feel quite sad

It's full of names of relatives and friends I once had.

But sometimes it makes me smile,

Reminiscing about times past –

I must contact those I haven't spoken to for a while.

Should I start a new book and remove many a name?

No, because eventually the results will be the same.

The Spinning Wheel

The spinning wheel and loom

Stood in the corner of a darkened room.

An old woman rocked gently back and forth in her armchair,

Her body bent, her feet bare.

Once she had sat at her spinning wheel every day:

Spinning threads of every hue

Made to be woven into wonderful cloth,

Just as generations of her family used to do.

Her family history lovingly told

In this way since times gone by.

Now her family were scattered all over the world –

The art of spinning and weaving the beautiful cloth was gone.

A tear trickled down as she thought of all this tradition

That had disappeared.

In Memoriam

Remember me with a smile,

For I was with you for quite a while.

Do not shed too many a tear,

For I have gone to join some of those I hold most dear.

Thank you all for coming here today

To see me on my final way

And for your love and kindness in the past –

The trouble is: life doesn't last.

So, remember me with a smile,

For I was with you for quite a while.

HISTORY AND POLITICS

Henry King

The chief defect of Henry King

Was overeating just everything:

Chips, burgers, buns, and anything sweet –

Very soon he couldn't even see his feet.

His family and friends, they feared the worst –

It happened one day,

He suddenly burst!

Poppies

In Flanders Fields the poppies in profusion grow, it is said,

The ground so fertile with the blood of the injured and the dead.

Some of those who died were just at the beginning of their life,

Cut down in a horrendous strife.

The First World War, the Great War,

The war to end all war.

No more war –

Is what they said.

I stood at the Tower of London and stared at the scene below:

A never-ending carpet of poppies,

Crimson red,

Planted there in loving memory and honour of the dead.

No more war –

Is what they said.

Umbrellas Are Not Just for Rain

He strode along the crowded street,

An English gentleman from head to feet.

His furled umbrella swinging on his arm,

His face smooth and very calm

Except those piercing eyes, darting everywhere –

Suddenly he smiled as he spotted a man standing over there.

The man was relaxed on the bridge looking at the scene below,

Mesmerised by the river's ebb and flow.

Our gentleman moved swiftly

And stood next to his prey –

The plunging needle point of his umbrella

Ensuring his victim never saw the light of another day.

Freedom

He marched up the road,

His banner held high,

Pointed towards the sky.

On it in large letters he had FREE DOM NOW

I marched beside him and said, *"Who is this Dom?*

And what has he done?

Please tell me, I don't understand

And I'm not the only one."

"I don't know," he said,

"I'm a Professional Peace Protester!

I make my own banners and go out every day,

Sometimes for pay."

I said, *"You might be a Professional Peace Protester,*

But you don't understand, and you can't spell."

With that, he hit me over the head with his peace banner

And told me to go to hell.

The Bad New Blues

I've got the Bad News Blues.

Brexit:

Are we or aren't we going to make a sensible exit?

Is Mrs. May for the chop?

Has Jeremy Corbyn lost the plot?

Are we going to have a fishing war with the French?

Is Mr. Barnier acting like a mensch?

I've certainly got the Bad News Blues –

Is there any good news to choose?

Oh yes – England won the cricket,

Although it was nearly a sticky wicket.

The Lift

The doorbell rang –

A young man stood on the doorstep

Wearing the biggest party rosette I'd ever seen.

"I've come to give you a lift so you can vote.

We like to look after our long-term supporters,

May I help you with your coat?"

I smiled and hobbled out to the car.

I enjoyed these occasional trips,

Although the polling station wasn't far.

I entered the voting booth

And held the stubby pencil in my hand.

Last time I had voted for the Monster Raving Loony Party,

This time I would be going Green –

No one would know – I couldn't be seen.

And you know what, at my age I don't feel mean!

Vote for Me

Vote for me

Whether you lean to the Left, Centre, or Right,

For I have a parliamentary seat within my sight.

I've already made you promises galore,

And I'm quite happy to make you many more.

Just vote for me.

The National Health Service is safe in my hands

I'll enlist more troops and send them all off to foreign lands

Trident missiles: we certainly need more,

Otherwise, what are those Scottish bases for?

Paternity leave for at least a year –

I can already hear you're beginning to cheer.

And when I retire from my parliamentary seat

I'd like to go to the House of Lords and join the elite

Where, I promise you, I will go in nearly every day

And sit and sleep, all on full pay.

CITY AND COUNTRY

<u>A City</u>

A city can be a lonely place

Sometimes you don't see a friendly face.

The sun rises, the sun sets every day

My nose to the grindstone – I have bills to pay.

Every day I go to work –

No time to relax, no time to shirk.

I pass homes and look through windows when the lights are on.

I see families together at work and play –

Perhaps this will be my life one day.

Belt Up

The woman I sat next to on the bus was on the phone.

She was speaking in such a loud voice

I heard all her conversation –

I didn't have a choice.

The young girl behind me was telling a friend

About a heavy first date.

All the bus was interested to hear how it ended –

We didn't have long to wait.

The man opposite had had a very bad day.

He was on the phone for a long time –

He had a lot to say.

The small boy in the pushchair was crying

And throwing his toys on the floor.

Each time his mother picked them up

He threw out a few more.

On that bus there was the most terrible din

So I stood up and shouted

"BELT UP!"

Suddenly you could have heard the drop of a pin.

I don't usually make a fuss,
So at the next stop I got off the bus.

The Onlooker

I am an onlooker in the Game of Life,

This is the way I avoid commitment and potential strife.

I peer through other windows both day and night,

Like a moth attracted to a welcoming light.

I walk alone on the sidewalks where there is no bustle –

This way I avoid humanity 'en masse' with all its hustle.

Will it always be this way?

Maybe a window in my soul will open up one day.

A chink of light is all I need:

To grow a flower, you need a seed.

Holiday Blues

Words cannot express the pure joy of standing barefoot

Watching the sunrise beyond the rolling green hills and valleys.

Day one of my countryside holiday –

What fun!

Then I felt the first drops of rain…

Thunder and lightning quickly followed on –

All the pleasure of anticipating the next two weeks was gone.

Oh yes, and I broke my toe –

Standing barefoot caused me woe!

Winter Blues

I've got those bad weather blues.

Just look out of the window or listen to the news.

The sky is grey

Nearly every day.

The outlook bleak –

The sun plays hide (but no seek).

Shall I build an ark?

The coming days look stark.

But there's a ray of hope:

I saw some spring flowers shyly poking through the earth –

Maybe this is the beginning of spring's birth.

Autumn Leaves

Fluttering gently to the ground, the autumn leaves fell.

Struck down by nature's cruelty

In their hour of beauty.

Red, yellow, green, and gold:

They lay in a carpet beneath the trees,

Gently fluttering and dancing in the breeze.

Suddenly it began to rain –

The skies grew dark

And a great gust of wind blew them all away –

A sure sign that autumn could no longer keep winter at bay.

Fireworks Night

Rockets soaring in a velvety sky,

Releasing a stream of coloured starlets from on high.

Catherine wheels whizzing round and round,

Needles of colour falling to the ground.

Bangers disturbing the peace of the night

Cats and dogs cowering out of sight.

Sparklers held in a gloved hand –

Keep an eye on that bucket of sand.

Potatoes baking in the fire

Which also serves as Guy Fawkes's funeral pyre.

Oh no! It's just started to rain –

Let's watch some telly until we can go out again.

Flying High

I am a 'High Flyer'

I aspire to be the best,

Watch me soar high above the rest.

The word failure is not one I know

To be second in life is far too low.

People look up to me as I pass them by –

For me, the limit is the sky!

What am I?

I am a kite.

I wave my tail gracefully as I pass out of sight.

HUMOUR

The Visitors

"*My, you do look well,*" they said,

As they settled themselves on either side of my bed.

They'd already put the grapes on a far-off table –

I couldn't have reached if I'd been more able.

They spoke to each other over my head

As my eyes bobbed from side to side of my hospital bed.

They spoke about where they'd been and who they'd seen –

I felt left out, it was very mean.

So I interrupted them and said, "*Good news!*

Yesterday I moved my big toe."

"*Sorry,*" they said, "*it's time to go.*"

And off they went!

Very Short Parodies

Water, water, all around and not a drop to drink.

That's because it's coming

From my neighbour's overflowing sink.

Shall I compare thee to a summer's day?

I've got bad hay fever, so please go away.

Shall I compare thee to a rose?

My face is red because of my runny nose.

This was the noblest Englishman of them all –

He drank, smoked cigars, and wasn't very tall.

Make me a willow cabin at thy gate,

This will ensure I'm never late.

Friends, voters, and countrymen,

I came to Bury A.V. –

Not to praise it.

Twinkle, twinkle, little star –

Don't go on X-Factor, you won't get very far.

If I was a rich man, I would find

A lot of women would love me,

But not for my mind.

Incy, wincy spider, climbing up the wall

If your name is Clegg,

Don't expect Cameron to cushion your fall.

Christopher Robin went out with Alice,

They didn't go to Buckingham Palace.

They went to Westminster Abbey and were charged £16 entry –

I think that was shabby.

On Yer Bike

I got my old bike out of the shed –

My family thought I was off my head.

I didn't want to go on a hike,

So I thought I'd ride my trusty old bike.

I cycle up hills and down dales –

One day I hope to get as far as Wales.

But when I cycle on the local cycle lane

The other cyclists say I'm a pain.

And as for the other traffic,

It goes so fast

And they shout rude comments as they go past.

Have they never seen an elderly lady on a three-wheeled trike?

One of the nicest things they shout is

"Get yourself a proper bike!"

<u>Wannabe</u>

I wanna be rich and famous,

I wanna be a TV star,

So kids will come to see me from near and far.

I can't tell jokes,

I can't sing or dance,

All I ask is give me a chance.

I wanna make lots of dosh –

So I can buy big houses,

Cars and expensive nosh.

I wanna be rich and famous,

I wanna be a TV star.

My Best Asset

Only one?

I have many more

For instance, there's my humility –

That's for sure.

My wonderful personality is there for all to see.

Wouldn't you like to be just like me?

My nature – so very sweet – I must stress

Just look at that woman in that awful dress!

I have patience by the bucketload –

"I'll give that woman a toot, she isn't fit to be on the road."

My sense of humour is sublime,

I never find anyone else's jokes as good as mine.

I just don't understand how I can clear a room so fast –

None of my friendships seem to last.

The Makeover

Mrs Cohen admired her fashionable tousled hair

And new retroussé.

In front of the mirror she struck a model-like pose:

The wrinkles in her face were disappearing fast –

She really hoped that Botox treatment would last.

Her breasts were now firm and pointed up,

A nicely rounded D-cup.

The tummy tuck had worked a treat –

The surgeon's cut was very neat.

Even her liposuctioned thighs gave her a thrill,

Although the treatment had made her feel quite ill.

Her bottom, once known as the family seat,

Was now much smaller, which was no mean feat.

"*Oh, Mr Cohen,*" she purred,

"*For you I've made myself young and beautiful, as you can see.*

Now, there's just one thing you can do for me.

From tomorrow farewell Mr and Mrs Cohen,

Welcome Mr and Mrs Chomeley–hyphen–Leigh!"

Whisper, Whisper

Whisper, whisper – don't speak too loud!

We don't want to be heard by any of that crowd.

See her, over there, from Number Four?

Well, strange men keep knocking at her door.

It's easy enough to see,

Child number four doesn't look like the other three!

Whisper, whisper – don't give her a glance

She'll be over on the borrow given half a chance.

Well, I must go – thanks for our lovely chat –

What do you mean, I'm "*a gossipy, spiteful cat!*"

Round the Block

She was a nice young girl who lived with her parents
In the house next-door the naval dock.
But now, she's been round the block, boys,
Yes, she's been round the block.

Those sailors wouldn't leave her alone, boys –
Even in her parents' home, boys.
Yes, she's been round the block, boys,
Yes, she's been round the block.

They made her promises they couldn't keep –
Even whilst her parents were upstairs, fast asleep.
Yes, she's been round the block, boys,
Yes, she's been round the block.

Now, you see that young woman walking along the road below,
With a cluster of children in tow?
Well, doesn't she look the picture of woe, boys?
And now she has nowhere to go, boys –
Yes, she's been round the block, boys,
Yes, she's been round the block!

LIVING IN LOCKDOWN

Eat Out to Help Out

Staycation is no vacation.

I mustn't moan –

Even though I'm home alone.

There is so much to be done,

But housework isn't generally fun.

I know,

I'll go and meet a friend.

We'll eat out –

£10 off is the newest trend.

Trouble with Your Bubble

I pushed open the door and entered the room.

The door shut behind me.

It was very dark.

All I could see was, in the middle of the room, a chair –

So I sat down there.

Suddenly, a bright white light shone on me

And a loud voice said,

"You're in a lot of trouble!

You haven't kept in your bubble."

I said, *"I only went out for a walk –*

I met someone I knew and we had a talk."

The voice said, *"The Thought Police are on their way –*

They've been watching you on Zoom every day.

Stand up! You're going for a ride,

And you'll probably end up inside."

The Future

I'm going to the opera at Glyndebourne

I've got my old ballgown out –

It definitely smells of mothballs,

About that there is no doubt!!

I'm going to Ascot,

I've got a big hat.

I understand there's horseracing,

But who cares about that!!

I'm going to the theatre,

We're going to sit in a box.

I shall wave at those down below

They will look up and think it's someone they should know!!

But that is all in the future –

Or is it in the past?

Meanwhile pass me the chocolates and the crisps

And turn on the T.V.

Tomorrow

The sun will shine all day.
The children will come home from school
And run out to play.

Neighbours will gossip over the garden wall.
Their dogs will rush around the garden,
Chasing an imaginary ball.

The weekend is here.

Tomorrow we'll go to the coast by car.
If we start out early it's not too far –
Or we might go to the theatre or cinema
By bus or train
We might go shopping and then out to eat –
A busy woman's weekend treat.

The shops are bustling,
Everyone is out and about –
Then I remember this was yesterday
Now we live our lives a different way.

What is the Question? What is the Answer?

What is the question?

What is the answer?

What is this life now COVID is here?

Can we still see and do the things we hold most dear?

Do not feel away from all you knew,

Your telephone can be a good friend to you!

Printed in Great Britain
by Amazon

82544417R00072